The Un-Common Raven:
one smart bird

By Diane Phelps Budden
Images by Loren Haury Photography

Red Rock Mountain Press LLC

Published by Red Rock Mountain Press LLC, Sedona, Arizona.
Printed in the United States of America.
ISBN: 978-0-615-73121-6.

Photographs Copyright © 2013 by Loren Haury, lorenhauryphoto@ earthlink.net or http://www.lorenhaury.visualserver.com/ Photos on pages 5, 14, 15, and 25 provided by author.

Acknowledgements
I am appreciative of the time and expertise provided in the review of this book by John Marzluff, corvid researcher at the University of Washington and author of several in-depth and fascinating books about crows and ravens.

The book could not have been published without the powerful, beautiful photos provided by photographer Loren Haury, who tells me he has well over 1,000 raven photos in his collection.

Emily Cory has been my raven muse these past four years as she willingly shared her knowledge of ravens with me, and, most importantly, her own raven Shade.

Dedication
A writer is only as good as her best supporters, so this book is lovingly dedicated to my husband Chuck, my special daughter Heather, and my two long-time friends, Mary and Barb.

CleanWatts Energy
Green-e CERTIFIED
Printed with *100% New Wind Energy*

Table of Contents

Juvenile ravens alert each other to the location of food, in this case, at the local KFC dumpster.

With its striking red rocks and brilliant blue skies, Sedona, Arizona, is one of the most beautiful places on earth, and I am lucky enough to live here. Situated in this nature's paradise, I am surrounded by mountains named for their shapes: Coffeepot, Giant's Thumb, Snoopy. Adding to the breathtaking view is beautiful Oak Creek that runs alongside Oak Creek Canyon as it twists and turns down the mountain.

After moving here, I couldn't help but notice the ravens circling overhead, calling loudly to one another. I watched them as they soared and dropped through the air, most often in pairs. They were Common Ravens, and they are anything but common.

I took a balloon ride that first year in town. As we lifted over the ground, my pilot pointed out deer and jackrabbits, and we began to talk about the ravens we saw. Turns out his daughter was involved in raven research for her graduate degree at one of the state universities. She believed ravens were smart enough to be used for search-and-rescue missions in the desert, and she had a raven called Shade that she was training.

That was the beginning of my love affair with ravens. I wrote a children's book, *Shade; a story about a very smart raven,* and realized I wanted to know more about these clever birds and share it with others. My experiences with Shade and the ravens in the wild led me to investigate the considerable amount of research about ravens, especially the groundbreaking studies of Bernd Heinrich and John Marzluff. Both of these researchers have published multiple books about the results of their work. See the "Learn More About Ravens" section for the titles.

The Un-Common Raven: one smart bird will make you smarter about ravens and, hopefully, curious to know more about this amazing backyard bird. My life has been enriched from my association with these wizards of the bird world. They are truly *uncommon.*

Diane Phelps Budden
Sedona, AZ

Where do ravens live?

Ravens have lived in North America for a million years or more. They came long before cave dwellers and their dog-wolves from what is now called Africa, after crossing the continent of Eurasia (Europe and Asia), and the Alaskan Bering Strait.

Some scientists believe that ravens might be descended from flying dinosaurs. Ravens did share a common songbird ancestor in Africa that split into perhaps three to four major types several million years ago.

As a species, ravens are labeled *Corvus corax*. They are part of the *Corvus* genus, and the Corvidae family, along with crows. There are forty-six species of crows and ravens around the world.

While the raven's best-known relative is the crow, the Corvidae family also includes blue jays, magpies, rooks, nutcrackers, and jackdaws.

There are ten species of ravens around the world, two of them in North America: the Common Raven, and the smaller Chihuahuan Raven. The Common Raven is the largest of all ravens and most prevalent in the United States. While crows and ravens share many physical characteristics, they also have obvious differences such as size and wingspan that allow us to tell them apart.

SCIENTIFIC CLASSIFICATION OF RAVENS	
Kingdom	Animalia (animals)
Phylum	Chordata (body skeletons)
Subphylum	Vertebrata (with backbone)
Class	Aves (birds)
Order	Passeriformes (perching birds)
Family	Corvidae
Genus	Corvus
Species	Corvus corax (Common Raven)

The raven's growth as a species is probably due to their ability to live and survive in a variety of climates all over the world. They have been able to spread to harsh climates like the Mojave Desert in southern California and the north slopes of Alaska by taking advantage of human food and water sources. In North America, they are predominantly in western and northern regions, both in low desert areas like the Sonoran Desert, and in western mountain ranges like the Rocky Mountains.

Ravens used to be more widespread in the United States, but centuries of being hunted as well as the growth of towns and cities, and the loss of forestland to agriculture, have reduced their numbers in the Eastern United States to a few states like Maine, Minnesota, Wisconsin, and Northern Michigan. They have also continued to flourish in the Appalachian Mountains. They are now making a comeback in various locations in Central and Southern United States.

RAVEN OR CROW?

Common Ravens	Crows
Weigh 2-3 pounds	Weigh 1 pound or less
Tails are long and wedge-shaped	Tails are shorter and rounded
Wingspan is 4-5 feet	Wingspan is 2-3 feet
Wings rustle in flight	No wing sounds
Totally black — mouth, beak, eyes, feet	Beaks are lighter colored
Shaggy hair on throat	Smooth throat
Long thick beaks	Shorter, thinner beaks
Ravens soar in flight	Crows flap their wings
Call is deep ("quork, quork")	Call is weak ("caw, caw")

© Diane Phelps Budden

9

The Migratory Bird Treaty Act of 1974 protects ravens. Several types of migratory birds--birds that fly between homes in the fall and spring--are protected from being hunted or captured. Even though ravens are not migratory birds, this law covers them.

Considered either a good or bad omen or sign, depending on the time and place, ravens have always fascinated humans. Their large size, flying and tool-making abilities, general cleverness, and sociability are impressive. While it's important not to use *anthropomorphic* words when talking about ravens--describing raven behavior as human-like--they do display some traits that seem similar to humans or our close relative, the chimpanzee. For this reason, there has been a great deal of research done on raven behavior that compares them to the behavior of other animals, including humans.

From Birds of North America Online, http:/bna. birds.cornell.edu/ bna, maintained by the Cornell Lab of Ornithology.

Year-round

This raven is caching meat in a hole in a tree and hiding the opening with Sycamore tree seed pods.

What do ravens look like?

Everything about mature Common Ravens is black: glossy black feathers that gleam in the light; black eyes; black beak; and black feet. Scientists believe that black feathers absorb more heat during the day, helping to add warmth in cold climates, besides blending with shadows in trees and brush.

They are large birds, weighing two or more pounds. Males are larger than females. They have four claws on each foot, three in the front and one in the back, that are well suited for grasping tree branches or tools they develop.

Ravens are as comfortable walking or hopping on the ground as they are flying, swaying from one leg to the other, and hopping forward or sideways. They are known to fly at speeds of 30-60 miles or more per hour. Typically, raven's wings are four to five feet long, which make for smooth sailing in strong wind currents. Raven watchers love the playful antics of these birds in flight: dropping

When winter comes, ravens rely on food they have cached or seek out animals killed on roadways or by other larger animals.

long distances in the sky; somersaulting in mid-flight; and performing other aerial acrobatics.

The raven's strong beak is equally impressive. It can rip and tear open almost anything. Hikers in the bottom of the Grand Canyon National Park have found holes in untended backpacks with the food removed! National parks have had to install a new type of trash container to stop ravens (and other wildlife) from picking open the lid to eat the food thrown away by humans.

Raven eyesight, while equal to humans, also allows them to see in more detail and variety of colors. They have a special, second eyelid called a nictitating membrane that can be used when they are resting or to communicate with other ravens. It also protects their eyes when flying in stormy weather.

A raven couple, perhaps on a short break from feeding the babies, are taking some time to allopreen.

Ravens have a large range of vocalizations or calls; at least 30 different calls with many distinct variations have been documented. They are the largest songbirds in the world. Each bird uses different calls in length, strength, and pitch or high or low sounds. Best known is the deep "quork, quork" call, with the males' call stronger than the females. Raven mates share calls to help identify their territory, and to keep track of each other when they are separated. They match their calls with postures and *gestures*, called "mating displays," to strengthen their bond.

The Cornell University Lab of Ornithology Macaulay Library provides an opportunity to listen to various raven calls on their website. You will also find instructions on becoming a "citizen scientist" in one of their many bird-tracking projects. (http://macaulaylibrary.org/index.do)

How smart are ravens?

Ravens are one of the smartest birds in the world, and rank in the top ten in intelligence among all living creatures, after humans, chimpanzees, and dolphins. They have a large brain compared to the size of their body, as do crows and parrots. Researchers at the Max Planck Institute for Ornithology outside Munich, Germany, believe ravens score about as high as great apes on various intelligence tests using *gaze-following* (able to follow where the researcher is looking or pointing), and problem solving.

Because of their exceptional intelligence, ravens learn quickly and have the ability to remember things. They are also very observant and curious about their environment. Self-awareness or the ability to recognize self and others, a trait of intelligent species, contributes to the sociability among ravens.

Another way that ravens demonstrate their superior intelligence is as a *toolmaker*. A species of crows in New Zealand regularly use twigs and other tools to extend their reach and obtain food. As part of an experiment at the University of Oxford in England, crows were offered food, but could not reach it with their beak. So they used a nearby stick provided by the researcher to pull the food toward them, sometimes making a hook on one end. Twigs are also used to dig out insects from a tree trunk, and to explore new objects safely. Ravens have also been observed near the ocean dropping stones in flight to crack open clams.

Well-known raven researcher Bernd Heinrich from the University of Vermont has studied ravens for many years and published several books. He explains that ravens have to fight other animals larger than themselves for food, and that probably requires quick thinking using *consciousness*--the ability to examine, evaluate, and make intelligent choices. In fact, Heinrich did an

Raven Research Study

Emily Cory, University of Arizona graduate student, took this series of photos to document her raven's performance on a research study. Emily wanted to show that ravens are capable of learning words and following commands. Shade the raven was told to go into the "test" room and find a certain toy. She did this many times under different conditions. While she did well following commands much of the time, of more interest to Cory was the fact that Shade intentionally retrieved the incorrect object when she was bored with the test. "Intentionally" in a non-human is a hotly debated subject among researchers. This might mean Shade has a higher level of cognition or mental process than just word learning and following rules.

experiment requiring ravens to use behavior not common for them. Perched on a branch, they had to pull up a piece of meat by a string attached to the branch. Since this was a new situation for them, they approached carefully. After some pecks at the string on the branch, and a few tugs, they gave up on the first day. But on the second day of the experiment, one of the ravens hauled up the string and got the meat within minutes. The others soon learned to copy this behavior.

Common ravens have also been observed tugging on the lines of ice fishermen to bring up the catch through the fishing hole. In addition, many raven researchers are impressed with the bird's ability to learn that types of human food might be a food source for them too.

Returning from a lucky hunt, this raven is headed back to his territory to cache this meat for another day.

This patient raven worked his way along the branch to grab the treat.

What's for dinner?

Ravens are *omnivores*, eating both animal and plant food. They are also considered *opportunistic scavengers*, eating whatever is available at the time. They clean up animals that have been killed in the road, known as *carrion*, scavenge in garbage dumps, and hang out at local fast food spots for bits of burgers and fries. They also like bird eggs (often stealing them from other nests), berries, nuts, insects, snakes, mice--whatever! If the meal is too big, ravens can break it apart into more manageable pieces, and fly off with it. Being clever birds, they also watch other animals or birds looking for food and join in the meal (or take it from them).

Before humans came along, ravens followed wolves in the wild to benefit from their hunting skills, eating the carrion of a dead animal after the wolves were through. Ravens needed the wolves to break through the tough hide of animals.

Constantly on the lookout for food, especially human food, this clever raven has snagged a Cheetos snack!

If needed, ravens can make the food they find easier to swallow. For example, ravens at Slide Rock State Park in Arizona regularly pick up discarded pretzels at the end of the day, and fly to a park water fountain to dunk them until soft.

Like some other birds and animals, ravens will *cache* or hide their food to eat later. Ravens have been known to re-cache their food if they think another raven has seen them at the first hiding spot. One raven, busy picking up scraps of food discarded by humans in a mall parking lot in the winter, quickly buried it in a nearby snow bank so the other ravens wouldn't see it. Wonder if the raven found it before the sun melted the snow?

This plump little guy has been searching for food in the snow. Maybe something he cached in warmer weather?

Ravens mate for life and can develop distinct communications and gestures as a pair. This affectionate exchange could also provide an opportunity for allopreening.

Do ravens have families?

Adult ravens mate for life. When they are about two or three years old, males will try to catch the attention of a favorite female through special calls, dances, and flying feats. Once the pair has chosen each other, they tend to settle in a home territory rather than fly distances or live with other ravens.

Ravens who mate use complex communications and display a high degree of cooperation. The pair will share certain "knocking" sounds, clicks, and screeches to defend their home territory. Cooing softly to each other, they *allopreen* or groom each other's feathers. Scientists say that allopreening is more common among chimpanzees and apes, but mated ravens have been seen picking through each other's head feathers with their beak. In fact, according to research done at the Max Planck Institute for Ornithology, ravens, similar to chimpanzees, use gestures to request preening from their mate. Once they are together, raven pairs stay together until one of them dies. The surviving bird eventually picks another mate.

The pair will build a nest together, usually in the highest fork of a tree or a safe perch in a cliff wall. They usually re-use a nest year-to-year by adding sticks and other materials they find. If a new nest is needed, the female will do most of the work. She builds one about the size of a laundry basket with an inner bowl-shaped space about eight inches deep, lined with soft materials like animal hair. It can take her two-three weeks to complete the job.

Once the nest is ready, the female raven will lay eggs within a week, usually six-eight blue or green blotchy eggs. She will sit on them, incubating them for 20-25 days, while the male brings her food to eat. Early in the spring

This fledgling's blue eyes and light-colored beak will turn dark within the first year of life.

This fledgling's nest is well protected from changes in the weather.

the eggs hatch, and the hungry babies open their red-colored mouths wide, crying constantly for food. Since there are usually six baby ravens per brood or hatching, the parents are very busy feeding them every few hours.

When they are born, the *hatchlings* are naked and orange in color, and can't see. At one week old, they are twice as large. Their eyes are functioning and have turned light blue. This is a dangerous time in their young lives as larger birds or animals may carry them off to eat. *Nestlings fledge* or leave the nest after they have learned how to walk and fly, usually when they are four to seven weeks old.

As juveniles, their eyes turn gray and their *plumage* or feathers is less shiny and metallic. They turn dark brown within the first two years of life and begin molting or shedding their feathers every year. The beak turns black during the first year of life and the mouth to gray, then black. Within two to three years, some will find mates and begin a family. Those juveniles that do not mate right away are usually part of a flock that roosts together and cooperates to find food.

How do ravens play?

Ravens are very sociable birds, starting with fellow fledglings, and continuing as juveniles who live and travel together. Researchers think the social bond formed between mated birds or groups of juveniles provides a way for them to exchange information about location of food so all can survive. Within the groups, there are *hierarchies* or ranked social structures, with one dominant bird that sets the rules for sharing food, and determines the acceptance of new birds into the group.

In the course of his studies, raven researcher Heinrich saw ravens playing in the snow. He thought they might be "snow-bathing," sitting down and flapping their wings, but they also slid and rolled down small hills, with other birds joining in. He has also seen ravens in his *aviary* or raven house hang upside down from a branch by one foot, with a piece of bark in the other foot that was passed back and forth between foot and bill before the bird flipped over like an acrobat and landed on the branch below. Other objects were used in this playful manner as well. Heinrich believes that this type of play may allow ravens to test behaviors and learn which ones are the best to continue using in the future to find food.

Raven antics while in flight are amazing to watch. They drop through the sky in quick turns, rolling end-to-end, speeding up as they pull higher. Often they can be seen flying in tandem with another raven, swooping up and down. They particularly seem to enjoy riding updrafts in the wind, rising and coming back down again and again.

Ravens seem to enjoy teasing one another or other animals as well. As fledglings they may play tug-of-war with leafs or sticks or wrestle over objects. As juveniles, they begin teasing other animals, dropping stones on them from the sky or stealing their food after distracting them. One angry squirrel was seen chasing two ravens up the road (had they found some of his food and made off with it?). When he had almost reached them, they flew off, the squirrel running after them, scolding loudly, the ravens answering in deep "quorks."

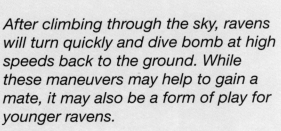

After climbing through the sky, ravens will turn quickly and dive bomb at high speeds back to the ground. While these maneuvers may help to gain a mate, it may also be a form of play for younger ravens.

Humans and ravens

Humans and ravens have lived together in North America for at least ten thousand years. Ravens learned that humans and their dogs were important to watch and follow because of the animals they killed. There were always scraps left behind to scavenge. Over the years, ravens were no longer considered pests, and instead became a subject worthy of research because of their amazing intelligence.

University of Washington wildlife biologist and Professor John Marzluff has studied ravens and crows over twenty years in the laboratory and in the wild. He is best known for his study about crow fledglings that he and his students put GPS trackers on in order to follow their whereabouts on campus. The mother and father crows yelled loudly at them, and even flew at them. Eventually, the crows recognized their faces. As they walked around campus, the crow parents would dive down at the students, cawing excitedly. They soon couldn't walk on campus without attracting these angry birds. Once Marzluff and his students wore masks over their faces to hide their identity, the birds no longer bothered them.

Another raven researcher, Emily Cory, based her graduate studies at the University of Arizona on using ravens as part of a search-and-rescue team in the desert. She obtained a raven from a licensed breeder, and when Shade was an adult bird Cory strapped a GPS tracker that was linked to her computer to the bird's back to transmit her movements during a search. Cory hopes one day to test her theory in the wild.

Meanwhile, new research is looking at Shade's ability to understand words and to respond to verbal commands. When asked, Shade can pick a specific object like a glove or stuffed animal out of a pile of objects and bring it to Cory. Shade's success rate in this research demonstrates her ability to understand some words and verbal instructions.

During an interview about his book *Dog Days, Raven Nights*, Marzluff said that his studies show a strong relationship has developed over the years between humans and ravens:

"I now see ravens and people as completely intertwined; as we affect them so do they affect us. We are in no insignificant part who we are because of our species' co-evolution with the raven."

It's easy to understand why researchers continue to study raven behavior and to document their intelligence, and similarities in their problem solving skills to other animals, even humans. Ravens are truly amazing birds!

In Red Rock country in Sedona, Arizona, ravens are year-round residents and much beloved by the locals.

Learn more about ravens

Cory, Emily Faun. (2012) "Rule Governance In An African White-Necked Raven (Corvus Albicollis)." Thesis. U of Arizona. Print.

Feher-Elston, Catherine. (1991) *Ravensong; a natural and fabulous history of ravens and crows*. New York: Jeremy P. Archer/Penguin.

Hassler, Lynn. (2008) *The Raven; soaring through history, legend, and lore*. Tucson, AZ: Rio Nuevo Publishers.

Heinrich, Bernd. (1999) *Mind of the raven; investigations and adventures with wolf-birds*. New York: HarperCollins Publishers.

Kerttu, M. E. (1973) "Aging techniques for the Common Raven (Corvus coxzx principalis Ridgeway)." M.S. thesis, Michigan Tech. Univ., Houghton, Michigan.

Knight, Richard L. and Call, Mayo W. (1980) *The Common Raven*. U.S. Dept. of the Interior, Bureau of Land Management.

Marzluff, J.M. and Angell, T. (2005) *In the company of crows and ravens.* New Haven, CT: Yale University Press.

Marzluff, John M. and Marzluff, Colleen. (2011) *Dog Days, Raven Nights.* New Haven, CT: Yale University Press.

Marzluff, John and Angell, Tony. (2012) *Gifts of the Crow: how perception, emotion, and thought allow smart birds to behave like humans*. New York: Free Press.

PBS Nature. (2010) A murder of crows. WNET.ORG Properties, LLC.

Savage, Candace. (1995) *Bird Brains; the intelligence of crows, ravens, magpies, and jays*. San Francisco, CA: Sierra Club Books.

Shumaker, Robert W., Walkup, Kristina R., and Benjamin B. Beck. (2011) *The Use and Manufacture of Tools by Animals*. Baltimore, MD: The John Hopkins University Press.

Glossary

Allopreen--process of cleaning and picking through the head feathers of another bird, usually a mate, to remove mites and other parasites.

Anthropomorphic--describing non-human forms, like animals and birds, as having human characteristics or behaving like humans.

Aviary--a large cage to house birds.

Cache--food hidden in a special place, usually in the ground, from other animals or birds, so it can be eaten later.

Carrion--dead animal in process of rotting.

Consciousness--being aware of one's own self and surroundings, of what one is doing, in relationship to others; important function for problem solving ability.

Fledge--ravens that have matured enough to leave the nest, usually six to eight weeks after birth.

Gaze-following--ability of a raven (or other animal) to see where a human is pointing using a hand or fingers in order to communicate with them.

Gesture--a movement of body or part of the body by ravens in order to communicate with another raven.

Hierarchies—a social ranking among a mob of ravens that dictates how food and space is allocated

Omnivore--eating both plant and animal life to survive.

Opportunistic scavenger--finding food wherever, whenever possible, eating all available kinds of food.

Nestling, hatchling--various stages of growth of a raven from birth (nestling) to living in the nest (nestling) until fledging.

Nictitating membrane--a second, transparent eyelid that ravens draw across the eye when sleeping or to communicate with mates.

Plumage--all the feathers on a raven's body.

Toolmaker--ability of ravens (or other animals) to make and use tools to obtain food.

Index

Diane Phelps Budden spent over 30 years in corporate and academic marketing before beginning her writing career, and self-publishing *Shade; a story about a very smart raven*. With this experience, she wrote and self-published *The Author's Concise Guide to Marketing: how to jumpstart sales of your self-published book* for first-time authors needing marketing skills. *Shade; a story about a very smart raven* was featured on NPR's *All things Considered*. Please visit her website to learn more: www.uncommonraven.com.

Loren Haury, a native Arizonan, retired to Sedona from La Jolla, California, in 1999 following a career in biological oceanography. He became interested in photographing ravens in 2004 after encountering them on many hikes in the red rock country surrounding Sedona. An ex-Navy fighter pilot, his admiration, and envy, were stirred by the raven's obvious love of flying and their consummate aerobatic skills. Photographing the incredible variety of their activities became his way of paying homage to these intelligent and charismatic birds.